DIVORCING THE ELECTRIC COMPANY

AN INSIDER'S GUIDE TO GOING SOLAR

BY SCOTT GORDON

Laguna Lantern Publishing Company

Published by:
Laguna Lantern Publishing Company
Laguna Niguel, CA 92677

USA * Canada * UK * Australia * India
China * Mexico * EU * South Africa

First published in the United States of America
By Laguna Lantern Publishing Company.

Divorcing the Electric Company copyright © 2015 by Scott Gordon. Cover layout by Evan Gordon.

Laguna Lantern Publishing Company supports copyrights. Thank you for buying an authorized copy of this book. Twenty-five percent (25%) of all profits are donated to charitable organizations that support humanitarian and animal causes around the world.

Laguna Lantern Publishing Co. ISBN 978-0-9963574-4-9

Printed in the United Stated of America

First Edition June 30, 2015

"There is no energy crisis, only a crisis of ignorance."

-- R. Buckminster Fuller

INTRODUCTION

So you're ready to file for a divorce from The Electric Company! You've had enough of high charges and cryptic billing structures! Delivery, generation, time of use, demand charges? Why does it have to be this hard? Well, I have some good news for you, it doesn't. As an 'enlightened' solar consumer (simply buying or downloading this book proves you are more enlightened than most), you'll get the best deal on your solar energy system and leverage it to the hilt for decades to come. You'll source the best product, from the best contractor, and finance it with the cold calculus of an investment banker (don't worry there's no calculus in this book ;). You'll have solar salesmen quaking in their boots when they realize you know more about their pitch than they do and save thousands or more in the process! You'll see through the scams and walk away with a renewable energy system that will work hard to save you money and make the planet a cleaner safer place for decades to come. Welcome to the Revolution! Let's get started.

TABLE OF CONTENTS

PART 1 — DISCOVERY
PART 2 — FILING FOR DIVORCE
PART 3 — THE SEPARATION
PART 4 — DIVISION OF PROPERTY
PART 5 — CUSTODY OF THE KIDS
PART 6 — REACHING A SETTLEMENT
PART 7 — THE APPEAL
PART 8 — SPOUSAL SUPPORT
PART 9 — RELOCATION & MOVE AWAYS
PART 10 — PRENUPTIAL AGREEMENTS
PART 11 — REMARRYING VS. DATING
PART 12 — SOLAR & YOUR FUTURE
GLOSSARY OF TERMS
ADDITIONAL RESOURCES

PART 1:
DISCOVERY

So you'd like to install solar panels on your home or business. Perhaps you've seen your neighbor put a system up on his roof or in his backyard, or you've been harassed endlessly by solar door-knockers and telemarketers, or maybe you read an article about solar energy that piqued your interest and you'd like to learn more about its benefits before you pull the trigger. If so, this book is for you.

Before we go any further, perhaps you'd like to know a little about the guy behind this book, how he got to be so versed in solar energy, and why you should listen to him. Well, the guy is me, and I got my start in solar back in 2006 when I began collection bids from solar panel installers for my home in California. I was what they call in marketing, an early adopter. Back in those days, Arnold Schwarzenegger's Million Solar Roofs initiative was in its infancy and my home was one of the very first to go through the California Solar Initiative Rebate Program.

In 2006, solar electricity was a foreign concept to most people and many of my friends and colleagues were skeptical about my decision to install the technology on my home and even more skeptical about my decision to become a solar salesman. My wife was the toughest of everyone to convince, and to this day, she stands as one of the hardest sales I've ever had to make (and I've made thousands).

She wasn't anti-solar, quite the contrary, but like many people, she was concerned that solar panels would be ugly. To her, the technology was expensive and might potentially ruin the curb appeal of our home – an unfortunately all too common occurrence today as evidenced by what I call the 'Tetris Train Wreck'. I'm sure you've seen it, the terrible looking solar installation that causes everyone in your neighborhood to gasp in horror whenever they happen by it.

Back in 2006, so little solar was installed that it was virtually impossible to drive her by any solar homes and say, "Look honey, it's really not that bad," or "Look there, you can hardly see the solar panels at all," or even "Look at that gorgeous installation."

Nope, back then, solar was unproven, expensive, and ugly – or that was the public perception.

It wasn't long after I had my twenty-seven Sharp 170 watt panels and SunnyBoy inverter installed that I called the company that sold me the system and asked for a job. To my surprise they hired me, and I had the pleasure of leaving my lucrative engineering career (and its comfy salary and benefits) to become a commission only outside solar sales guy at a tiny solar startup based in Fallbrook, CA called HelioPower. Nearly a decade later, I'm the company's President.

With nearly 5,000 commercial and residential solar systems under my belt, I've learned a thing or two about solar energy and everything that goes along with it, and I'm going to share much of what I've learned with you. In this book, I'll discuss how to select the right equipment and contractor for your job, the ins and outs today's solar finance models, the federal solar tax credit, long term care and feeding of solar systems, common pitfalls to avoid, and a host of other topics that will make you a solar salesperson's worst nightmare – well hopefully not, but after reading this book, you'll know more than 99% of the solar salespeople working at big box stores, relentlessly knocking on your door, or hammering your home telephone number night after night.

Armed with this knowledge, you'll not only get the best deal, you'll get the *right deal* – a custom tailored solar energy system that is financed correctly (for your needs), cash flow positive, and virtually maintenance free for decades to come. You'll divorce The Electric Company and be free from their naggingly high and often enigmatic charges.

So, where to start? Well, there's no better place than Discovery. After all, every divorce starts with Discovery. It's the process of obtaining the information you need to defend your interests and get the best settlement once the divorce is finalized. When shopping for solar, the more time you spend in Discovery, the better off you'll be as your divorce from The Electric Company shakes out.

For starters, you need to know if you're a good solar candidate. Believe it or not, solar doesn't work for everyone. Some roofs are too small, too shaded, and too old. Some electric bills are too little or have painfully long ROIs (returns on investment). How do know if solar is right for you?

First, you need to have an open and unobstructed roof or area (could be a field or hillside) that receives lots of direct sunlight. An area that faces the equator is best (this is south for those of us located in the Northern Hemisphere), though east and west roofs are ok if they are all you have available. North is a no-no!

Your roof should also be in good repair. This means that it will not need replacing anytime soon because once you install a solar system on it, a roof tear-off and replacement gets a lot more expensive. When in doubt, have a reputable local roofer conduct a thorough inspection and make any necessary repairs before you get any solar bids.

Additionally, some roofs require extra care when considering solar. These are: clay, slate, wood shake, lightweight concrete, and other brittle roofing materials. If you have a brittle roof, ask how the solar company intends to water seal it. There's nothing like a leaky roof to rain on your solar parade.

Having a big electric bill is usually a qualifier for solar power. In my experience, solar begins to make economic sense when you pay The Electric Company a minimum of $150 per month. It also desirable that your ROI (return on investment) is less than eight years. Anything longer than that deserves additional scrutiny, and don't take the solar salesman's word for it. Do your own math.

Over the years, I've seen example after example of shady solar contractors 'dressing up' their customers' (victims') ROI. Some popular techniques include (but are not limited to):

> 1. Underestimating or discounting the impact of shading from trees, chimneys, or other obstructions. Shade can have a dramatically negative effect on solar energy production. The more shade you have, the longer your ROI.

2. Basing solar production on a south facing roof when in fact their client's roof is east, west, or even north!
3. Overestimating the annual increase in electricity costs from The Electric Company. A fair and conservative estimate in my experience is 4-6%. I've seen disingenuous salesmen use 30% or more. This particular scam makes your ROI appear fantastic when it is in fact, fantasy.
4. Using all three of these deceptions at once on the same bid. If your ROI is unrealistically fast (like less than one year) and your savings absurdly high (like $10,000,000 for a 5KW system – yes, I've actually seen this), chances are the solar salesman is intentionally deceiving you.

If you want to be a savvy solar buyer, you need to be informed, not only about solar ROI, but about how you and your family consume electricity. The ROI you'll get from energy efficiency often dwarfs that of even the best solar system. In my years of selling solar panel systems, I can't recall the number of times I've asked a client how he was using electricity only to get a response that sounded something like this: "I don't know, like $200 per month," or "I don't know, my wife pays the electric bill."

Notice I asked 'how' *NOT* 'how much'? See the difference? The sad reality is that most home owners can't answer the first question at all and only make a guess at how much. The 'how' is far more important than the 'how much'. Why? Understanding *how* you use electricity can guide you to discover myriad ways to become more energy efficient.

But why would you want to become more energy efficient? After all, aren't you going solar so you can use as much electricity as you want without the hassle and pain of high bills? Hopefully not, because more efficient buildings use less electricity (and other fuel stocks) and therefore require fewer solar panels to 'zero out' their associated electric bills, and isn't that ultimately your goal? – To save the most money for the least amount of out-of-pocket investment? I imagine that's why you've chosen to read this book. It was certainly my intention in writing it.

Let's begin with a quick solar economics lesson. In 2015, the average cost of installing a single solar panel (panel, inverter, racking, wire, conduit, building permits, etc) was $1,100. The average wattage of a solar panel was 275 watts (a far cry from my 170 watt panels!) therefore, one kilowatt of solar power costs about $3.64 per watt or $3,640 ($3.64 x 1,000 watts). It then follows, that for every kilowatt you reduce the size of your solar system, you reduce its cost by $3,640.

Even if you are only able to reduce your system by a single solar panel, you will save an average of $1,100, making your ROI on this chapter alone is 10,911% (based on a purchase price of $9.99)! But these savings are just the tip of the ROI iceberg.

I'd like to share with you how I applied this principal to my own home. When I first looked into solar, I was told that I needed a system that would produce around 1,000 kilowatt hours of electricity per month on average. This amount of electricity required six kilowatts worth of solar panels. At

$8.32 per DC watt in 2006, I was looking at $49,920 before incentives!

This high price tag was far beyond what I had budgeted for solar and I was highly incentivized to examine *how* my family was consuming electricity.

I immediately researched and ordered $300 worth of CFL lightbulbs (which have since been upgraded to LEDs) and two energy efficiency books. I changed all the lightbulbs both inside and outside my home and implemented several of the strategies I learned from reading those two books. The result? I reduced my monthly consumption by over 400 kilowatt hours and reduced my solar system size from six kilowatts to four.

In 2015, using this very same strategy could save you $7,280!! In 2006, with solar prices much higher than they are today, it saved me $16,640! In either case, that's a lot of cash. Now there's an ROI!

I can cite example after example of cases where I saved my clients so much money with the energy efficiency techniques I taught them, they decided not to go solar. While I may have lost a few sales, I ultimately gained many strong references and made a big difference for many families struggling to save money who couldn't afford solar at the time.

I cannot overemphasize the importance of getting efficient *before* going solar. I hope this section has inspired you to invest the time necessary to truly understand how you are currently using electricity in your home and to research tactics that will be most effective in curbing your monthly energy consumption.

As a part of this exercise, closely examine your electric bills. Sit down with a year's worth and wallow in them. Compare winter and summer. When do you use more? When do you use less? Where are spikes? July? January? What do you think is causing them? Air conditioning? Pool pumps? Are there cheap energy efficiency solutions that would address the issues?

You may notice two very common electricity spikes on your annual bills. The biggest usually happens in the heat of summer (air conditioning as you probably guessed) while the shorter days of winter require more lighting (both practical and holiday festive) and the possible use of electric heating. How might one attack each of these spikes individually?

If you live in a climate where night time temperatures are significantly lower than daytime temps, a whole house fan will probably knock out 70-90% of your summer air conditioning bill. Significant can be as little as 15 degrees, but whole house fans work best when the delta is more than 20 degrees Fahrenheit. Likewise, if you change out those old Christmas lights for newer LED strings (along with the rest of your lighting), you'll reduce your lighting bill by 80% or more yet not miss a minute of holiday cheer.

These changes are simple examples of more cost effective methods to lower your electric bills significantly without solar panels (and more importantly don't require expensive and time consuming building permits and city inspections!). Yet even after you deploy energy efficiency strategies in your home, you will still end up using some amount of electricity, therefore solar will play a role in your divorce from The Electric Company, just a smaller less expensive one.

Think of it like settling your divorce in arbitration versus taking your grievances all the way to trial. Regardless of the outcome, the second option is always more expensive – every time, all the time. Energy efficiency pays and it pays BIG, so do your research, implement your findings, and be prepared to save thousands. The only losers in this deal are The Electric Company, who will receive fewer of your hard earned dollars, and the solar salesman, who will receive a smaller commission as a result of your energy prowess.

It is often said that knowledge is power. When it comes to solar, knowledge saves power, and saving power saves you money – lots of money! During the discovery phase of your divorce from The Electric Company, you'll need to learn everything you can about how you use electricity and how to employ energy efficiency strategies to get your consumption under control.

Mastering the Discovery phase of your divorce will save you thousands of dollars and possibly tens of thousands of dollars on your solar system. On the other hand, skipping this step will, well, do I really need to say it?

PART 2:
FILING FOR DIVORCE

Well the big day has come. You've had enough! Your marriage to The Electric Company has been a one way relationship for as long as you can remember. But what do you do? You can't just divorce The Electric Company, can you?

Well, the short answer is yes, but...

To truly divorce The Electric Company, you'd need to live completely off-grid, and while that sounds romantic to some, I promise you, it's not all it's cracked up to be. Living off-grid means counting kilowatt hours to make sure you don't deplete your batteries, having a back-up generator on standby in the event you do (with fossil fuel reserves to boot), and praying none of your equipment decides to break at any point along the way (because it might). Living off-grid, while quite doable and admirable, requires a certain amount of grit and perseverance found in only a minority of people – preppers, hippies, and hermits.

Most of the people I've interacted with over the years have no idea where their electricity comes from and they honestly don't care. They just want to plug their (insert any highly addictive electricity sucking device) into a wall socket and go on with their lives. They couldn't be bothered, and while there's nothing inherently wrong with this, it doesn't lend itself well to an off-grid existence.

Some of you may be thinking "but Scott, what about those super awesome Tesla batteries? For $3,500 I can live off-grid forever can't I!"

Ummm, no you can't. Today (July 2015) there are two models coming to a garage wall near you – a 7kWh unit and a 10kWh unit. Most houses I've looked at (literally tens of thousands since 2006) use somewhere between thirty and fifty kilowatt hours a day on average. Let's take a home that uses 42 kWh per day for our purposes here and see if the 7kWh unit is up to the challenge. We'll call this our 'average home'.

At a minimum, our average home would need three 7 kWh units just to be on par assuming that half of the electricity is used during the day and half at night (it's rarely this clean a split in real life). However, a savvy consumer would buy a fourth unit in the event there are multiple days of rain *OR* some other weather event that impacts solar production *OR* they experienced a day where they consume more electricity than average (say they have out-of-town guests crashing at their house) *OR* temperatures become extreme and thus they require more electricity to keep the dwelling comfortable, either warm or cool.

Let's see, that's four units at $3,500 each or $14,000 for starters. But these units don't operate in a vacuum. You still need to buy power electronics (charge controllers and the like), hire a contractor, pull permits, pay sales tax, and install a backup generator in case all else fails (let's price this item at $6,000). Using conservative figures, you're looking at $25,000 or more <u>*PLUS*</u> the solar system (which will need to be oversized to accommodate both the large battery bank and the extra electricity necessary to power your home while charging that large battery bank).

All this extra money, and you're counting kilowatt hours. Not so romantic sounding anymore, is it? But don't be downtrodden my eco-friendly compatriot, there's still a useful place for a Tesla battery if you must have one. You can use it for backup power in the event of a blackout. Since most blackouts last only a few hours, a single seven or ten kilowatt hour unit should suffice the majority of the time. If you experience blackouts more frequently or for longer periods, do yourself a favor and buy a nice backup generator instead. The technology is tried and true and costs up to 80% less than today's lowest cost battery solutions (think of rows of golf cart batteries occupying your garage), and will last much longer.

PART 3:
THE SEPARATION

So far you've learned that energy efficiency pays big dividends and that off-grid living is both inconvenient and expensive (regardless of the hype), and you're now thousands of dollars richer because you've used this knowledge to significantly reduce your electricity consumption, and by extension, the solar system required to power your home, but there's still more to learn, a lot more...

While not quite as absolute and final as a divorce, a 'grid-tied' separation from The Electric Company is like having a friend with benefits. In other words, you eliminate your electric bill, but still get to use the electric grid as a backup at night, during rainy/snowy days, or when hosting those energy hogging out-of-town guests I mentioned earlier. In this example, think of the grid as your virtual battery.

There's tremendous value in having the electrical grid at your beck and call, and it's not to be underestimated. Today's grid is truly a modern marvel! My home has solar panels on the roof and is connected to the grid (in an arrangement commonly known as 'grid-tied'). My electric bill averages $30 a month (some months it's as little as $5). Yet if I didn't have solar, my bill would be $300 - $400 per month, so essentially I'm enjoying a 90% discount over grid rates while still enjoying 100% of the electric grid's benefits. Sweet deal, right?

So here's your starting point, a 'grid-tied' solar system that saves you tons of money AND gives you full grid benefits. We can always 'pimp' our system out later if we wish (with batteries and the like), but let's start where 99.9999% of solar customers start and end – at grid-tied.

First, let me give you a definition of grid-tied solar. It's as simple as this: a solar energy system that generates credits by day (by spinning the utility's meter backward) and debits by night (by consuming the day's credits). The value assigned to the day's credits determines your return on investment (ROI) commonly defined as the time period in which the solar system pays for itself.

In my experience, payback can be as little as four years and as many as fifteen years depending on the cost of electricity and whether rates are flat (all you can eat at a fixed cost per kilowatt hour) or tiered (each level costs more than the last – in other words, the more kilowatt hours you use, the more each one costs).

Think about this for a moment. How many other home improvements have an ROI? How many other home improvements have you moved ahead with only after they've first proven their ability to pay you back? Probably none. Sure, we've all justified kitchen and bathroom remodels as adding value to our home, but we never see that money until we sell our property and even then it's a crap shoot. It's not like your new granite countertops are paying rent.

On the other hand, solar panels pay rent every month for decades *AND* they add value when you sell your home. My solar panels pay me $300 a month to 'rent' my roof. The only other improvement that is in the same league as this is a granny flat or something similar that can be rented out for monthly cash flow. Of course, unlike solar savings, rent collected from a tenant is generally considered taxable income.

Thus, when we consider solar panels from an ROI standpoint, grid-tied solar is the most logical (and economical) place to start. All it requires is four basic components: solar panels, inverter(s), racking (something to attach everything to), and the balance of system (referred to in the industry as B.O.S.) – this is the copper wire, electrical conduit, circuit breakers, etc. In this setup, there are no expensive batteries, charge controllers, or backup generators to worry about. Your goal is to 'spin the electric meter backwards' and rack up credits to use as you see fit – generally at night or during dark winter months.

Simple right?

It can be if you know what you're doing. Let me give you some basic rules to follow when selecting equipment (we'll cover contractors and financing later) so you get the right stuff from solid 'bankable' manufacturers:

> 1. Only select a solar panel manufacturer with diversified holdings and a strong balance sheet (in other words, choose a company that doesn't only make solar panels. Examples are: Mitsubishi, LG, Hyundai, Sharp, Kyocera, etc). The one

exception is SunPower. They make excellent panels and have the backing of the world's fifth largest oil company – Total S.A. You're looking for a solid company that will be around to honor the standard 25 year warranty. That's a very long time, so choose well. Sure, there are lots of pure play solar panel manufacturers and many of them make excellent quality products, but this is about more than quality, it's about longevity. What are the odds that the company be around 25 years from now? If it is not, what will this mean for your warranty? That's an easy one: no company = no warranty. Simple rule: if you haven't heard of the panel manufacturer or the solar salesman says, 'the panels don't matter', consider this a big red flag.

2. Inverters are much more important than solar panels. That's right. Please read that first sentence again. So, what are

inverters? Inverters are the devices that turn DC (direct current) into AC (alternating current) and interact with the electrical grid. They are the brains of the operation. Your home/business and every electronic device therein runs on AC, so inverters play a crucial role in converting solar power into usable power. The higher the efficiency of the inverter, the more electricity you get to keep. Today there are three architectures that dominate the marketplace: String, string/optimizer, and micro-inverter. There's a lot of debate among industry experts about the best architecture and each has its advantages and disadvantages, so I'll share my preferences based on thousands of successful solar installations. If you have no shade and a beautifully sunny location, a string inverter (SMA is my favorite manufacturer because of their products' legendary reliability) are the way to go. They are easy and inexpensive to install. If shading is a concern, string-optimizers and

b. Do you flash the penetrations? How?
c. How do you seal the penetrations?
d. How do you seal pilot holes and nail holes in the event you pull up tiles?
e. What brand of racking are you proposing for my project?
f. Why has your company selected that racking vendor?
g. When do you think I'll need to replace my roof? (<u>never</u> install solar panels on a roof you think may need to be replaced within the next five years. You will live to regret it).

Inverters and electrical panel tie-in's also deserve their share of pointed questions. After all, we are dealing with electricity here and we need to treat it with the respect it deserves. You don't want an electrical fire, do you?

Here are some questions that will keep you from making some rookie electrical mistakes that some disingenuous solar contractors bank on:

1. Will my current electrical panel be sufficient to accommodate your proposed solar system?

2. If 'No', ask: How are you planning to address this? Common options are:
    a. Upgrade to a larger electrical panel (an expensive but sometimes necessary option).
    b. Derate your main breaker - a cheaper but less desirable option than upgrading since once you derate your breaker – say from 200 Amps to 150 Amps – you may experience 'nuisance trips'. These are events are triggered when you use too much juice and the whole house powers off after the main breaker trips. I lived in an old farm house in college where this was and all too common occurrence. Take it from someone who's lived it, nuisance trips get super annoying super-fast. Make sure if you go

down this road, the solar company conducts a 'load analysis' to determine if nuisance trips will be likely after you derate your main breaker. WARNING: Many shady contractors are derating breakers without telling homeowners in order to cut corners and save money. Don't let this happen to you!

c. Line Tap – This method 'lags' the solar inverter output into The Electric Company's side of the service. This can be a good money saving option if your electric company allows it, many don't. If in doubt, call the customer service number on your electric bill and ask.

3. What happens if the electricity turns off? Unless you have batteries, the answer should be 'your solar panels turn off'. If the answer differs dig deeper. SMA offers a smart plug that allows you to run small

appliances and devices during a power outage, but this feature is very limited and not considered a whole house backup by any stretch. Untrained or deceptive salespeople will represent the 'smart plug' as such. Don't be fooled.

Next we need to select the right contractor. If you've been diligent about asking the questions I've posed so far in this book, many of your solar suitors will have been eliminated or self-selected out (to pursue easier prey, no doubt).

Sometimes, it's hard to know what's worse, buying a car or buying home improvements. Let's face it, we all have some fear around being ripped off by used car salesmen and contractors. The 10 o'clock News regularly exposes some shady contractor running off with customer deposits and leaving a disastrous mess of broken homes in his wake. It's either that or some fast talking car salesman unloading lemons from Hurricane Katrina onto unsuspecting widows.

It's no wonder the general public approaches these transactions with trepidation, but in my experience, it's not terribly hard to select the right contractor if you know what to look for. Here are my rules:

1. Go with the trusted reference – hire the highly recommended contractor who did a good job for you friend or neighbor. This is the safest choice from a quality and integrity standpoint.

2. Be very cautious about buying anything from someone who knocks on your door. That's not to say that door to door canvassers are all evil, many reputable companies market this way, but if you elect to do business with one of them, it's always advisable to do a little extra homework to protect yourself and your roof.

3. The same is true for the telemarketers. To expand on this a bit more, 'the government' is <u>NOT</u> 'giving away free solar panels' compelling 'you to act now before pending legislation ends this fantastic government program.' Lies, all of it. Hang

up the phone and block that number. If they keep calling you, report them to the FTC (especially if you're currently on the do not call registry). A couple of $10,000 fines should get them to leave you alone!

4. Always get two additional bids. This will keep the referenced guy honest and give you negotiating power if you can find a better price for the same thing. You get your guy and your price. Cha-ching – you're officially a savvy solar customer. I've seen this trick shave thousands of dollars off the price of solar without sacrificing an ounce of quality.

5. Make sure your chosen contractor is licensed and insured and uses their own employees to install your solar. Many solar telemarketers and door knockers sub-contract their installations to the lowest bidder. If you choose to move forward with one of these, make sure they are licensed in your state and perform

their own work. The last thing you want is uninsured day laborers drilling holes in your roof and running high voltage electrical wire. The practice of subcontracting labor is far more common than you may believe, and low priced subs will cut every corner they can to make a buck in this highly competitive corner of the solar industry.

6. Check that the equipment offered meets the criteria laid out above. If not, but you like the contractor, ask him if he can provide the equipment of your choosing at the same price point.

7. Ask for addresses of other local installations they've done. Drive by and see them. Make sure he's not installing Tetris Train Wrecks.

8. Speak with a few references (a step most customers skip). Ask to talk with some clients that have had solar for a long time

(five or more years) to assess how well the contractor's work stands the test of time. Are they experiencing roof leaks or other problems? This exercise is a really good test of the quality of the contractor's roof sealing practices, wire management, and B.O.S.

9. Did I mention to be cautious about buying solar (or anything that isn't Girl Scout Cookies) from someone who solicits you? Solicitors aren't always there with your best interest at heart. They typically have a quota to hit and are hoping you will help get them there. The salesperson you want to do business with is a consummate professional, one who you can count on to answer the phone when you have a question or a problem down the road. If you are solicited and the deal looks good, make sure you ask for and check the salesperson's/company's references. If they can't provide them, move on.

That's pretty much it. You can also tack on some of the traditional stuff: a list of local customers whose projects you can drive by and see in person (I can't overemphasize this), online reviews (Angie's List is the best I've found since reviews are by real customers - not shills, disgruntled ex-employees, or competitor's looking to discredit), longevity in business, and so on. For my home improvement projects, I always go with the local contractor who is known for his quality work and integrity.

I'm willing to pay extra for quality and a solid reputation. I've repaired enough solar systems installed by low bidders to know going with the low priced contractor is a very bad idea. The cheap guy either doesn't know how to bid the job correctly, is willing to cut corners, is using inferior products (generally B.O.S. – e.g. the stuff you don't see), or is learning how to install solar on your house – truly the nightmare scenario. Maybe even all of the above.

Choosing a reputable contractor with strong references will always beat the ad you clicked on, the direct mailer you received, the listing in the yellow pages (do they still print those?), or the mystery man shadowing you in the aisles of Big Box Hardware.

Once you've selected your equipment and contractor, you'll need to pay for your solar system. If you're paying cash, great! You'll get the best deal and the quickest ROI. If you're financing your system some other way, some serious homework is required to protect yourself from getting a raw deal, especially if you've decided to go with Dealer Financing (the financing a solar contractor may offer you).

Solar financing covers a lot of ground and can take many forms: traditional bank loans, home equity lines of credit (HELOCs), same-as-cash schemes, leases, ppa's (power purchase agreements), and property tax secured loans (referred to as P.A.C.E – property assessed clean energy). Navigating these waters can be quite treacherous for the uninitiated. Don't get ensnared in a bad finance deal. Read on!

PART 4:
DIVISION OF PROPERTY

UNIT 4

IMPACT OF ROCIETY

If you decide to buy your system outright (with cash), the division of property is simple, you own everything (solar panels and associated equipment) and the utility and finance company get nothing. You are now officially your own electric company with a customer of one – you. Congratulations! Solar ownership is a winning model if you've selected the right equipment and contractor.

Otherwise, if you've chosen to finance your solar, you'll need to wade through a sea of finance options from loan products based on home-equity, fico scores, and property tax assessment to leases and ppa's (power purchase agreements). Which option is best for you? How do you avoid getting ripped off? What happens downstream if you sell your home?

Fear not. I'm incredibly comfortable navigating the solar financing jungle and I know where all the landmines are buried. Stick with me and I'll teach you the tricks of the trade only solar insiders know. The information presented here is some of the most valuable in this book and mastering it will save you lots of money, hassle, and time.

P.S. My lawyer made me write this next part:

You own your financing decisions and the contracts attached to them. This information is for illustrative purposes only. If you are confused or have financial or tax questions – please consult a licensed financial planner or tax advisor.

In my experience, the next best thing to paying cash for your system is taking out a home improvement loan. When I went solar, I paid for my system with a HELOC (home equity line of credit). This type of loan nearly went extinct in the aftermath of the mortgage crisis, but was an incredibly effective way for me to buy my solar system back in the mid 2000's.

For my family, a HELOC made tremendous financial sense. My electric bill at the time was $220 per month. I used my Wells Fargo home equity line to buy my solar system and the monthly payment was $158 per month. After taking the home mortgage interest deduction on my Federal Tax Return, it was closer to $100 per month.

So there I was saving $120 per month using OPM – other people's money. Instead of blowing that $120 a month on whatever, I pretended that Wells Fargo was my new utility, and continued paying them $220 per month.

The beautiful thing about a HELOC is that as you pay down principal, your monthly payment goes down too. $158 soon became $150 and eventually $100 and so on, yet I continued paying $220 a month. That, plus sending them my entire federal tax credit (which I received the following year), made it so I paid the entire loan amount off in 5.5 years.

It's been 2.5 years since I paid off my HELOC and every single month since then my solar panels have paid me $250-$300 like clockwork. That's a car payment for most people! Maybe it's groceries for you, that extra contribution to your kid's college fund, or some additional padding for your nest egg. Whatever you decide it is for you, IT'S TAX FREE!

Think about that. After taxes, you'd need to earn $500 a month to pay an electric bill of $300 a month. If you do what I did, you're getting that money as tax free savings with 100% of it going into your pocket. What a deal!

Fortunately, for those who qualify, this form of lending is making a comeback as the Great Recession fades into history. If you have equity in your home, a decent fico score, and would like to enjoy low payments, possible tax write-offs, and low or no closing costs, it may be worth talking with your bank about a HELOC. In my opinion, it's the best way to pay for solar. Look what it did for me! Again, talk with your tax advisor about any potential tax benefits.

While you're meeting with the loan officer, ask if the bank offers any solar specific loans (a popular option at credit unions), home improvement loans, cash out re-fi's, and the like. Check out all of your options before you settle on a loan product.

After cash, a bank loan is the best way to buy solar, just be sure that your loan payment is lower than your electric bill (25% less is a good target), and be sure to include any interest related tax write-offs in your savings calculations. As always, and I can't say this enough, get any presumed tax benefits blessed by your financial planner or CPA.

P.A.C.E. – also known as Property Assessed Clean Energy – allows homeowners (and businesses) to finance energy efficiency improvements secured by their property taxes. Along with leases, these are the financing vehicles most often misrepresented by the robo dialers ("We're calling from the government with free solar"), but this class of loan has many advantages. The first is that you can finance more than just solar electricity. P.A.C.E. approved equipment includes (but is not limited to):

1. Solar Electric Systems
2. Solar Thermal Systems
    a. Swimming Pool Heating
    b. Interior Water Heating
3. Heat Pumps
4. Energy Efficient Air Conditioning and Heating
5. Whole House Fans
6. Energy Efficient Lighting Upgrades

7. Artificial Turf
8. Variable Speed Pool Pumps
9. Electric Vehicle Charging Stations
10. Fuel Cells
11. Weatherization, Insulation, Ducting
12. Small Wind Turbines
13. Cool Roofs and Radiant Barriers
14. Energy Audits
15. Attic Fans
16. Biomass Furnaces
17. And much more!

P.A.C.E. is a good option for those who have more than one energy efficiency project they'd like to pursue, have equity in their home, have had their accountant review and bless their eligibility for realizing the tax advantages unique to this class of financing, ditto for the federal solar tax credit, and lastly, don't wish to encumber their credit score with a large debt (most P.A.C.E. loans don't require a FICO score to qualify and don't show up on FICO scores as debt since they are considered a tax assessment similar to Mello Roos).

P.A.C.E. loans aren't available everywhere so you'll need to investigate local market conditions before getting too far down the road. A quick internet search should turn up any providers in your area. Some of the most popular in California are HERO, yGrene, and California First.

Staying in the loan realm, the next group of financing products are those offered exclusively by solar contractors. These loans <u>ARE ALWAYS</u> more expensive than any loan you can get on your own from your local bank. Why? High closing costs and fees (up to 18% of the loan value on some products I've seen) plus high interest rates and payment accelerators (yeah, you read that right) conspire to make this class of loan products a place to wade very cautiously.

I'm not saying all these products are bad, I'm just saying Caveat Emptor (buyer beware). You'll need to ask a lot of questions to protect yourself, such as:

1. Are you building dealer fees (closing costs) into the price of the system?

2. If so, how much are these? (They can be up to 18% of the balance on 1.99% & 2.99% interest rates.)

3. Does my loan payment have an accelerator or escalator? How much is it? (Would you really sign a loan where the payment goes up every year? I certainly wouldn't.)

4. What is the term of the loan?

5. Are there any pre-payment penalties?

Let me spell this out for you. Many solar contractors are offering tantalizing 1.99% and 2.99% loans. Many of these carry an 18% 'dealer fee' to buy down the interest rate (why do you think it's so low?). Now for some quick math using a $25,000 solar electric system. An 18% dealer fee on such a system would be $4,500. This amount is tacked on to the price of the solar system before determining your monthly payment. Thus, if you choose this type of loan, your solar system will actually cost you $29,500 instead of the original $25,000 plus interest.

In order to slide the dealer fees by you, your contractor will likely focus your attention on the low monthly payment and low interest rate. The payment may still be attractive, but consider securing a no cost HELOC instead and save yourself a bundle.

If your contractor is offering you a 'same-as-cash' loan (and I have a very low opinion of these) ask:

1. The questions above (same-as-cash loans have high dealer fees), plus:

2. What happens if I have a loan balance at the end of the term?

3. What's the interest rate after the 'teaser' period? (often 20% or more)

4. Is the interest rate applied against the starting loan balance, totaled, and added to the remaining principle at the end of

the 'teaser' period?

5. What is the interest rate on the new balance? (see line 2)

This is very simple. If you don't have the cash in the bank (or some guaranteed way of coming up with the cash before the end of the 12, 18, or 24 month 'teaser' term), you are taking a tremendous risk with a 'same-as-cash' style loan. While the allure of 'same-as-cash' sounds great when the salesman is pitching it, I would advise against divorcing The Electric Company for this mistress of the night. If you're not careful, she'll break your heart and leave you broke at the altar.

I once received a phone call from a gentleman looking for advice on his same-as-cash solar (S.A.C.) loan. He had signed up for this loan (with another contractor who wouldn't answer his calls) to finance his federal solar tax credit. Unfortunately, the gentlemen didn't qualify to take the full tax credit. He had earned less money the previous year and therefore paid less taxes. When his refund arrived, it wasn't enough to pay off his

S.A.C. loan. This is one reason getting professional tax advice is so important!

He used what he received ($2,000) to pay his S.A.C. balance down to $7,000, but when penalties, fees, and back interest kicked in at month thirteen, his balance popped up to $13,000 (from his original principal balance of $9,000)!

Unfortunately, there was nothing I could do to help this poor gentleman. He had been taken by a fly by night 'Pete in the pickup' who had long since vanished, but not before saddling his client with financial contracts that were legal, binding, and punitive.

I've always advised my clients that financing their federal solar tax credit with a same-as-cash loan is a fool's errand. Don't allow yourself to be talked into going down this treacherous road.

With that, we enter solar lease territory. Welcome to the Wild West! While this method of solar financing has its proponents, there are significant risks to consider before divorcing the electric company for one of these beautiful vixens.

The generic solar lease sales pitch goes something like this: "Are you tired of paying too much for electricity (of course you are, who isn't)? Would you like to pay less (well, duh)? And lock-in those savings for the rest of your life (yup)? Would you like to enjoy all these benefits with no money down and 'free' installation (who wouldn't) and a production guarantee? Ok then, all you need to do to start saving right away is sign here, we'll take care of the rest!"

Sounds too good to be true, no? The reason many companies LOVE leasing is that it's a "one call closer's" dream come true. If you've heard this pitch, you probably thought it sounded very appealing – you get all of the benefits (save money, 'free' installation, money back guarantee, 'free' maintenance, easy transfer) and none of the hassles (paying for it, maintenance headaches, lost production).

In addition to all of the other benefits offered, leasing companies will often try to lure in consumers with offers of cash back, prepaid credit cards, and other 'fleeting' discount schemes. The offers usually sound like this:

'Receive $1,000 cash back if you sign up for free solar by September 30th!' September 30th soon turns into October 31st and then November 30th and so on as the promotional advertisements are simply updated on the first of the subsequent month to attract the next round of unsuspecting prospects.

Where do you think the money for these promotions is coming from? Do you really think you're getting $1,000 cash back for free? It's baked into the deal, and you're paying it back with interest!

I view the lease/ppa as a pre-nuptial agreement that must be contemplated very carefully before divorcing The Electric Company and getting remarried to one of these 20 year contracts.

Here's a list of items that the solar leasing guy who won't give you a moment's peace at BigBox Hardware isn't telling you (and sadly probably doesn't know himself) about solar leases:

1. The lease's 'production guarantee' *may have a few loopholes written into the contract* such as:
    a. If you don't clean your panels, the guarantee is null and void (forget what the sales guy said about 'free' panel cleanings – probably won't happen).
    b. The 'free maintenance' you're being offered is just the leasing company's way of taking advantage of manufacturer warranties that come 'for free' with your solar equipment. The very same warranties you'd get if you bought the system outright.
    c. Keep your trees trimmed or you can forget about any refunds for low solar output.
    d. Keep your internet connected to the leasing company's monitoring equipment or else…
    e. And a few other hidden gems lurking in the fine print of the

lease/ppa contract you're being asked to DocuSign. These items can generally be found in the section of the lease/ppa contract entitled 'Customer Responsibilities' or something similar.

2. Your roof penetration warranty might be *as little as one year!* Some leases offer five, but a couple of the big guys offer only one year. Think about it, if your roof starts leaking 367 days after the installation, you're out of luck. THIS IS THE SINGLE MOST IMPORTANT ITEM ON THIS LIST – it's the roof over your head! Water leaks can be devastating, especially the long slow ones that mold, mildew, and dry rot thrive in. Ask:
    a. All of the roofing questions I posed earlier in this book, plus:
    b. What is your roof penetration warranty?
    c. Where can I find that in the contract?

d. What happens if I get a roof leak?
   e. Do you have a service department staffed with technicians?
   f. What kind of response time are you contractually obligated to provide your customers in the event of a roof leak or other service issue?

3. Transferring your solar lease may not be as straightforward and easy as represented by your salesperson. What if, for example, you've receive a cash offer for your home from a foreign national (say from Canada or China) who doesn't have a FICO score? Such an offer would likely require you to buy out the remaining lease in order to sell your home. Are you prepared to do this? By prepared, I mean are you ready to fork over $20,000, $50,000, or more if your buyer doesn't qualify to assume your solar lease? What if the buyer of your home is averse to leasing and wouldn't

even consider leasing an automobile? How might this effect your home sale? What other complications might exist down the road if you need to sell your home? The chapter entitled **Relocations and Move Aways** is dedicated to this topic.

4. What if the person buying your home has a different energy profile than you? Let's say you are a huge consumer of energy (electric car, three kids, AC running all summer) and the buyer of your home isn't (a single guy who travels for work all the time and is rarely home). There's a very high likelihood that this guy won't eagerly assume the $300 monthly solar lease payment on your grossly oversized (from his perspective) solar system. It's a much different story if the solar just 'comes with the house' (i.e. you own it). He'll probably gleefully rush out and buy a Tesla Model S P85 to soak up all that 'extra juice' his 'free' solar system is

throwing off and kiss his gasoline bill goodbye.

5. Your monthly/annual savings are not guaranteed. Production is (sort of – see exclusions above and in your contract). Please, read that again. This means that if your consumption habits change (and they often do) so will any presumed savings. Kids moving home from college, getting a Nissan Leaf, elderly loved ones moving in, installing a swimming pool, and dozens of other life changes can equal electricity consumption changes in the UP direction. Doing the opposite can equate to changes in the DOWN direction. Locking in your electricity rates works better for UP than DOWN (see my example above with the single professional buying a home from a large family). The problem is that lease pushers are trained to 'sell savings not equipment', so when a customer's energy profile changes, and it often can, the

savings evaporate and the customer is left angry and confused.

Finally, what if your local utility restructures rates as is now being proposed in California? Have you signed up for a rate that may put you on the wrong side of this restructuring? In other words, could you end up 'upside down' on your solar lease payment? Sadly, the answer is yes, especially if you've locked in a high payment with a high accelerator.

6. Your 'fixed' rate, might not be fixed after all. It may, and likely does, have an annual payment escalator. This means that each and every year, your lease/ppa payment goes UP and that is bad! If you choose to sign a lease, make sure you are truly locking in your payment (or kilowatt hour price if you're signing a PPA). After all, Albert Einstein famously said, "The power of compound interest is the most powerful force in the Universe." Check

your contract for the escalation rate (typically 2.9% or 3.9% per year) and cross reference that to the schedule of monthly payments (usually toward the tail end of the contract) to confirm that you're not getting ripped off. By insisting on a non-escalating lease, **you will save thousands of dollars** over the term of the agreement and protect yourself from an undesirable 'upside down' lease payment down the road.

7. We're your new utility! Let me ask you, when you embarked upon your mission to divorce The Electric Company, were you looking to rush into the arms of another monthly electric bill or did you wish to become your own electric company? Is it better to deal with one electric company or two? Pursuing this course of action is akin to divorcing your spouse in order to marry his slightly less overweight twin while keeping your ex waiting in the wings. Crazy, right?

Becoming your own utility gives you larger savings and increased flexibility now and in the years ahead. All of the solar system's benefits accrue to you when *you own* the solar panels. A solar salesmen pushing the lease is hoping to lock you into a 20 year agreement with a 3.9% payment escalator and another utility to deal with when something goes wrong for the purpose of earning a higher commission.

8. The solar equipment doesn't matter because you don't own it. This one is easy, it's a sales ploy. Neutralizing the equipment discussion eliminates a boatload of customer objections and significantly speeds up the sales process. As I mentioned earlier, solar leasing salespeople are taught to 'focus on savings not equipment' since this results in more 'one call closes' (a lot more, it's a sales manager's dream come true). But here's the deal – you should care, an

awful lot, because someday you or a future buyer of your home will own this equipment. Quality of product and bankability of the manufacturer over the long term (25 years+) matters! Don't get caught making this common mistake. Of course, if you've read this far, you already know why equipment matters, but, nonetheless, it's worth repeating.

9. You could be stuck holding the bag on _their_ solar system. When you sell a home complete with a solar system you own or have financed traditionally, the real estate transaction is not needlessly complicated by the solar panels. They're just another home improvement that adds value, and any outstanding loan balances are paid off in escrow. When you introduce a solar lease into the mix, you are rolling the dice. If there's a loser in the deal, it's quite likely to be you. Don't get caught. If you think you might move in the first five years of the lease,

you're taking a big risk by signing one. More on this later.

10. Check your lease documents carefully to see if you are able to add solar panels to the system later or incorporate new storage technologies (like Tesla's and Samsung's home battery packs). Most leases do not allow either of these items to be added later while others specifically exclude them. So what if you'd like to add panels or batteries later? Many leases will put you into contract default if you add any equipment whatsoever to *their* system without their permission (which they are unlikely to give you, by the way since your system has long been sold off to investors). You may have locked in your low, low monthly payment, but you've also locked in your technology and what you can do with it now and in the future.

11. Fannie Mae and the FHA agree that solar systems installed under a solar lease or ppa cannot be included in the official valuation of a home for mortgage purposes. To the contrary, they mandate that solar systems owned or traditionally financed by the homeowner must be included in the valuation. I guess you get what you pay for... I encourage you do explore this in more detail online if you're curious. There are numerous articles on the subject.

Wow, that's a lot of information for someone not to be telling you! But if they told you everything I've laid out here, you probably wouldn't sign up, and certainly not with someone over the phone or standing awkwardly in your doorway. Look, the intent of a solar lease is to make a $40,000 commitment as easy to 'buy' as an impulse item at the supermarket checkout line, maybe even easier. So while you still might consider a solar lease, at least now you're going in with eyes wide open. I almost feel bad for the solar salesman about to pitch you one of these (ok, not really).

A solar lease is ideal only under three conditions:

1. You are not eligible to monetize (take) the Federal Solar Tax Credit (ask your accountant whether this applies to you).

2. It is pre-paid (you pay for all 20 years of electricity upfront MINUS the Federal Solar Tax Credit) – Pre-paid leases can be a good deal. They are my preferred leasing vehicle. I would consider one of these for myself if I couldn't take the federal tax credit. Combining a prepaid lease with a HELOC is an interesting strategy for those without a tax appetite.

3. The reimbursement rate for lost production (your Production Guarantee) matches the true cost of the electricity you're buying from The Electric Company (e.g. alimony) in the event their solar system fails or under produces.

All three of these conditions should be met before proceeding with the lease deal. Otherwise, ownership is a better option for most.

One last thing concerning Division of Property involves The Electric Company. You may own your house and the property it sits on, but The Electric Company owns the utility meter and all of the electrical that feeds into it from the street.

You own the circuit breaker panel and all the electrical infrastructure going from that box to the rest of your home and property. You can do whatever you like (so long as it's permitted, up to code, and installed by a qualified electrician) on your side, but you may never, under any circumstances, touch The Electric Company's side due to high voltage and other dangers. Consider this a restraining order you must obey or find yourself in contempt of court with the fine being severe injury or death.

PART 5:
CUSTODY OF THE KIDS

When The Electric Company supplies us with all of our electricity, most of us never give it much thought until the power goes out, and then it's one of the most inconvenient of today's conveniences to forego. Fortunately, the grid overall is highly reliable and affordable. It's just that solar electricity is cheaper when it's produced and consumed on site.

If you've ventured this far into your solar journey, it's likely that you are close to finalizing your divorce with The Electric Company, and you're about to get custody of the kids – those wonderful solar panels, and everything that goes along with them. No need to fret though, these kids are practically self-raising.

If you've remarried a lease, then you'll have to grant visitation rights to the solar leasing company. The good news is, they won't drop by very often, usually only to repair their solar system or repossess it if you stop making your child support payments (i.e. lease payments), but since their visitation rights are legally recognized (as a property lien), when you sell your house, they'll only be willing to remarry a buyer they like (high fico score) and who is willing to grant them the same visitation rights you agreed to originally. Visitation rights (read: Lien) will also muddy up your home's title and throw up red flags on title searches. I guess the upside is that the leasing companies provide childcare (solar monitoring systems) and child support (production guarantees) in exchange for visitation rights.

If you've purchased or traditionally financed your solar panels, you'll need to know how to raise them into the finest electric bill fighters the world has ever seen. This starts and ends with keeping them in prime fighting condition.

First, understand your area's soiling conditions. What's soiling? It's what happens when dirt, soot, and other particulates collect on your solar panels. The more soot they collect, the unhealthier your solar panels become until they are smoking two packs a day and hanging out at the tattoo parlor. Clean them at least once per year (I recommend using a licensed window cleaner) or more if you live by a freeway, in dusty area, or near a construction site.

Next, make sure you have your solar monitoring hooked up and that it's operating properly. Your monitoring should be configured to send you alerts in the event of a system alarm or failure. It's also helpful if your contractor is setup to receive system alerts. This will enable his service department to respond quickly to any service and warranty issues that arise.

It's a major bummer when the solar system fails and no one notices! It can be very costly. I once had a customer who disconnected their monitoring for a year (accidentally they claim). It cost them over $1,000! How? The solar circuit breaker tripped and no one noticed until their annual 'true-up' bill arrived in the mail. Ouch.

Monitoring is the solar equivalent of parental controls and babysitting. If anything goes wrong, you'll know instantly, get your 'kids' the attention they need, and be back online quickly and efficiently thereby mitigating any potential financial losses.

A few years after my solar panels were installed. I noticed a strange pattern on my daily solar reports. My system came on as usual, but at 1pm it shut off for a couple of hours, then came on again, and later (around 4pm) shut off again. It did this the next day, and on the third day, I went out to my SunnyBoy 3800 inverter to see if I could figure out what was going on.

Turns out my kid (SunnyBoy) was winded and needed an inhaler. Upon closer inspection I discovered that the intake fan (which keeps the unit cool) was clogged with soot (from my clothes dryer vent above it). The lack of airflow was causing SunnyBoy to overheat. This excess heat triggered a safety feature which shut SunnyBoy down to cool it off and preserve its sensitive electronics.

The fix? Believe it or not, I simply vacuumed out the fan with my ShopVac and like magic the inverter began working beautifully again. I now perform this routine maintenance twice a year and haven't had a single issue since. Imagine if I hadn't been alerted to the problem, not only would I have lost money (production), but I would have likely burnt out my inverter.

Other than keeping your solar panels clean and cared for, there isn't a lot more to solar upkeep other than protecting your panels from solar bullies. Who are the solar bullies? In a word – foliage (trees, bushes, vines, etc). We have a saying in solar – 'go solar, kill a tree'. I know it sounds terrible, but shade is a real solar electricity killer.

To keep the bullies from beating up your 'kids', you'll need to keep them trimmed and as far away as possible from the panels. If you keep the solar bullies at bay and your panels clean, they'll put even more money in your pocket year after year and for decades to come.

The best news is that you'll never need to put these electric bill fighting wunderkind through college (even as they're contributing to your 'other kids' college funds).

PART 6:
REACHING A SETTLEMENT

Depending on where you live, there may still be charges associated with connecting to The Electric Company's grid. In some areas, the electric utilities are lobbying to increase charges specifically for solar customers. They claim that solar customers are unfairly subsidized by other rate payers and are in essence grid freeloaders.

As a result, they are advocating for monthly hook-up fees of anywhere from $5 to as much as $50 per month and flattening tiered rate structures to disincentivize would be solar customers . These facts shouldn't dissuade you from going solar. Over the course of its useful life, a solar array will produce very cheap electricity (assuming you bought it right – the entire point of this book!). The average cost of the electricity it generates should be down in the $0.08 to $0.11 per kilowatt hour range (this is what the leasing companies mark up to make their money).

Since solar energy is strongly supported at the local, state, and federal levels it's unlikely The Electric Company will get much support from elected officials in raising fees exorbitantly. Let's face it, there's value in connecting to the electric grid.

Since over 99% of solar is grid-tied (connected to the grid) most solar today is generally net-metered. This means that the excess electricity generated during the day and during the high production summer months is stored as credits on the grid. These credits are used at night and in the winter to offset lower solar production. This arrangement can best be compared to a squirrel saving nuts.

At the end of the year, usually defined as the anniversary date of the day your solar panels went live, you settle up with The Electric Company. I like to think of this as paying alimony. This is your 'true-up' bill. It's made up of the net balance of your credits (what you produced) and debits (what you consumed). If you produce more than you consume, you have a credit (minus hookup fees), but if the balance goes the other way, you get a bill. And if you're not paying attention, it could be a big one!

I once had a customer who lived in a large Tuscany style home on several acres in wine country. The customer contracted with us to install a large 15 kilowatt ground mounted system on a slope below the house. The system was designed to offset nearly 100% of my client's electric bill. We installed the system, did a beautiful job, our customer was extremely happy, fairy tale ending? Not quite...

A year later, my client's true-up bill arrived right on time, only instead of having the credit they were expecting, they had a debit, a bill for $14,000! As you can imagine, my once happy customer was fit to be tied. They called my office demanding that I reimburse them for 'the full amount' since 'it was obvious the solar system wasn't working'.

As it turns out, the solar system was working. Not only was it working, it was working splendidly. The solar panels were producing 15% (nearly 3,200 kilowatt hours) *more than expected*! So what was the problem?

After the solar installation, my client bought a Chevy Volt. The Volt, while significantly reducing the family's gasoline bill, consumed over 3,200 salesman overestimated the annual production either through ignorance or deception. I've seen grossly negligent overestimates of 40% or more!

Keep the solar contractor honest by double checking his numbers against a state or federal solar estimation website. There are many available such as CSI-EPBB in California and NREL's U.S. solar calculator. Many states have their own sites. A quick online search will turn up ones local to you.

Be careful of look-a-like sites posing as government resources. These have begun to proliferate the internet with the sole purpose of capturing your personal information and selling it to the highest bidder (usually a motley crew of solar contractors hungry for fresh leads who will then proceed to robo-dial you nonstop for weeks on end).

Make sure you enter in your zip code (if they ask for more than this, it's probably a poser site), the direction the panels are facing (south, east, or west – north is bad if you live in the Northern Hemisphere), tilt (the slope of your roof or the intended installation angle for flat roofs and ground mounted arrays), and any nearby shading (trees, chimneys, roof lines, etc) to get an accurate estimate. If you're not comfortable doing this yourself, no worries, simply ask each of the salesmen to demonstrate how he arrived at his estimate. If he doesn't know, disqualify him. Knowing how to determine production estimates is solar 101. If he can't complete this simple task, what else doesn't he know?

To summarize this section, it's important that you understand your annual production estimate, stay within your annual kilowatt hour budget (unless you're ok paying an electric bill), and confirm that the estimate you're signing off on is accurate and the salesman can demonstrate it is thusly so to your satisfaction.

PART 7:
THE APPEAL

So just when you thought your divorce with The Electric Company was settled, they've decided to appeal! What exactly does this mean? As we look out into the future, The Electric Company will need to find new ways to generate profits and pay dividends to its shareholders. If you believe it will sit idly by as the solar industry steals all of its customers, you got another thing comin'.

Like all power plants, solar is a long term commitment. As an enlightened solar consumer, you will take the long view of this lucrative investment. Know that The Electric Company has all sorts of plans to get you back as its customer. This section covers what it has up its collective sleeve and strategies you can use to hit their curve balls out of the park.

The Electric Company's new pricing structures revolve around that lovely smart meter they installed on your home or business in the last few years. If you don't have one of these digital beauties yet, have no fear, there's one with your name on it arriving soon.

Smart meters allow The Electric Company vast new insights into how and when you use electricity and allow it to charge accordingly. The following list covers some of the most popular new billing methodologies, but I'm fairly certain these represent just the tip of The Electric Company's creative iceberg.

1. Time of Use – Also known as TOU, charges different rates based on the time of day and the time of year. Most often it is comprised of 'Peak' day and summer rates and 'Off Peak' night and winter rates. Savvy solar customers can leverage TOU in a major way. More on this later.

2. Demand Charges – This class of charges is well known to commercial customers already. Demand charges are basically surcharges for using a bunch of kilowatts at once. Let's say for example that you come home from work on a hot summer evening. You may need to cook dinner, run a load of laundry, charge your cell phone(s), watch television, run the

dishwasher, and, of course, cool down your oppressively hot house. If you were to do all of these activities in a 15 minute period (captured thanks to your smart meter), you would suck a ton of juice *all at once*, and BAM you have yourself a Demand Charge. What might this look like on your electric bill? Let's say you spiked 15 kilowatts in that 15 minute window. Your monthly bill would show 15 kilowatts multiplied by some factor, say $5.00 per kilowatt. In this example, your charge would be $75.00 for that spike. On some commercial electric bills I've seen, that charge is $25.00 per kilowatt. Whoa, Nellie!

3. TOU + Demand – This one is a real challenge. In essence, 1 + 2 = 3, only worse. It's the worst of both worlds wrapped up in a present you'd never want to open. This new type of billing structure takes TOU (day/night - summer/winter kWh rates) and adds

demand charges (On Peak/Mid Peak/Off Peak/summer/winter per KW surcharges). Net, net, you'll be billed for spikes happening at high demand times (like a hot summer day at say 5pm) *and* those happening at lower demand times (like winter evenings). The good news is that the demand rates will be lower during lower demand windows. The bad news is that your energy consumption can spike at night when your solar system is off. Solar systems can help with demand if weather permits. In other words, if it's cloudy for 15 minutes at 2pm on a Wednesday in July, and you happen to spike, that charge can follow you up to six months on some tariff structures I've examined. Solar can help reduce demand charges, but weather is the big wild card here.

4. Generation vs. Delivery - The Electric Company breaks the power it supplies to your home down into these two

categories. There is a cost to generate the electricity at the power plant and a cost to deliver it to your home over the grid. It's quite possible that by lowering generation costs and raising delivery costs, The Electric Company could get some of their solar customers paying more every month. Take a look at your most recent electric bill and see if your local electric utility is separating generation and delivery charges. The upshot here is that the most expensive times to deliver electricity generally coincide with the highest solar production times (summer days). Site delivered solar power can be quite valuable in this scenario.

5. Monthly Hook-up Charges - The Electric Company believes that there is value for solar customers when they connect to the grid (and I happen to agree). After all, it's the place you store your kilowatt hour credits and it acts as your battery at night

and during other times when your solar panels might not produce optimally (winter, rainy days, etc). It's nice to know the electric grid is there for you when you need it. As we move into the future, The Electric Company will charge increasingly more for the privilege of using the grid as your virtual solar battery. My electric company currently charges $4.95/month, and I consider this to be an excellent value. I don't expect it to stay this cheap forever, but I'd be willing to pay much more for this convenience, maybe even up to $50 a month (remember my bill would otherwise be $300 a month). Not every solar customer agrees with me on this subject and many rightfully argue that connection fees never factored into their ROI calculations when they decided to install solar in the first place. They view hook-up fees as a betrayal or illegal tax. The point is, like it or not, connection fees are a reality and you should understand how they work. The good news is, if you do solar right and do it soon, hook-up charges will be of little concern to you.

Covering five newfangled billing methods should suffice in communicating my point. I simply wish to demonstrate that The Electric Company is cooking up all kinds of ways to remarry you. They're like the psycho ex you can't shake. But don't fret, there are ways you can protect your solar investment.

Here are some tactics you can leverage to maintain your grid independence:

1. Keep your electricity consumption under control and within budget – see Chapter Six.

2. Determine if time of use (TOU) works for you. Many of my solar customers use very little electricity during the day while their solar panels are cranking out tons of extra kilowatt hours. My savvier clients will sell these 'extra' kilowatts hours back to The Electric Company at expensive day rates and buy them back at cheaper night

rates.

I recently had a customer who switched to TOU after buying an electric car (recall my Volt example above?). While he's consuming more kilowatt hours than his solar kicks out, he's charging his car (and running just about everything else he can) at night and he has a net metering credit! Yes, he's still married to the utility, but he's able to see other people, and maintain his *benefits* while being paid alimony. You'd hire that attorney, right?

3. If and when demand charges hit, you'll need to learn how to 'stage' turning on appliances and other electricity hogs. Using the example above, rather than come home on a hot day to a baking house to crank out all your chores, you'd instead turn your AC on from your smartphone app as you leave the office, make dinner when you arrive home, run your dishwasher a bit later, and save the washing machine and dryer for bedtime,

thus spreading the energy loads out over a longer period of time. As your appliances become 'smarter', they will be able to handle much of the timing tasks for you. Scary? Maybe. Convenient and money saving? Absolutely. Products like Google's Nest are counting on it.

Of course, if you'd prefer not to tango with The Electric Company you can choose to go completely off-grid. This is the kind of divorce where there is no joint custody, visitation rights, alimony, or appeal, and it's expensive as all go get. As I covered earlier, off-grid systems are expensive, and I hate to burst your bubble, but you're not living off-grid very comfortably with a single $3,500 Tesla Powerwall or other equivalent device.

The average household would need to spend upwards of $25,000 on batteries, power electronics, and a backup generator (a must if you plan to live comfortably and by modern standards). This is in addition to the solar panel system, which needs to be sized larger to accommodate the rigors of off-grid living.

Having said this, I've seen some really cool off-grid setups. There's a gentleman who lives on The Big Island of Hawaii who has one of the coolest off-grid systems I've ever seen. He has an 80 kilowatt solar system that feeds into a lithium ion battery system (of data center quality). When the batteries are charged, he overflows the excess electricity to a hydrolyzer where he uses it to split hydrogen and oxygen atoms from water (remember when you did this experiment in high school chemistry?). He then uses the hydrogen to power his fuel cell car and other equipment. Truly awesome! For as little as $500K plus, you could enjoy the very same setup.

I am hopeful that as batteries become cheaper, systems like the one I just described will become a reality for all people, just as cellphones and laptops with internet access have. This is, in fact, Elon

Musk's stated goal for Powerwall and devices like it.

My hope in writing this section is to give you confidence that your solar decision is/was a good one regardless of what happens with utility rate structures. By going solar now you save money immediately and still have plenty of options moving forward (especially if you own it).

The really good news is that utilities and governments are slow moving entities, and a decision to go solar now will likely result in you getting 'grandfathered' into the current structure. While they debate, you save money, and as far as I'm concerned, they can debate until the cows come home. If the situation ever gets to a place where you want to pull the plug altogether, you can always go off-grid – if you dare… evil laugh…

PART 8:
SPOUSAL SUPPORT

In every divorce, the topic of spousal support inevitably comes up. Commonly known as alimony or patrimony, the court decides who should support whom in the aftermath of the breakup.

Again, the only way to truly 'divorce' The Electric Company is to go entirely off-grid. Anything short of that and you'll still have to pay some sort of spousal support. This can be anything from monthly connection fees to demand and delivery charges.

Depending on the severity of these fees, you may not care all that much, especially if they are inconsequentially small like the $4.95/month I currently pay. Others reading this book may feel very differently regardless of the severity of the charges. Either way, unless you go completely off-grid, you'll be paying something for the privilege of using the electric grid.

As I relayed earlier, there is tremendous value in using the grid as your virtual battery. I'd much prefer spending $4.95/month for my virtual battery than a lump sum of $25,000 or more for a physical one. As battery backup systems become more affordable over time and financing becomes more readily available, the economics of this technology should improve. Until that time, connecting to the grid is a major bargain by comparison.

Spousal support takes on another form as it relates to the solar leases of the world. Let's face it, you didn't divorce The Electric Company intent on marrying the first suitor that came along, did you? Your new squeeze may appear cheaper out of the gate, but you may have signed a 'pre-nup' that provides for a 3.9% cost of living increase (payment escalator) each year for the next twenty of your new marriage, and if it doesn't work out, the cost of your second divorce could be in the tens of thousands of dollars.

If your 'Ex' (The Electric Company) lowers or realigns rate tariffs (collapsing tiers and leaving 'peak shaver' customers potentially upside down on their solar lease payments), you may want to go rushing back into her waiting arms, except you can't because you've signed a pre-nup with the leasing company, and you'll pay them their pound of flesh regardless. Tough luck.

Sadly, your only option at this point may be to default on your lease obligations, but doing so will likely trash your credit, so I don't recommend this course of action under any circumstances.

With your Ex on spousal support (remaining tiers of electricity, hook-up fees, etc) and your new hubby charging you more every year plus a huge break-up fee if your second divorce goes badly, you're stuck between a rock and a hard place.

In my opinion, the fewer spouses you are supporting, the happier you'll be in the long run. You'll save more money with fewer hassles, surprises, and complications.

PART 9:
RELOCATION & MOVE AWAYS

Luckily, I've been married to my lovely wife for nearly two decades and have never been divorced, but from my observations of folks suffering under the weight of multiple divorces, the second one is usually a lot tougher than the first.

This is certainly true of solar leases and ppa's. Let's say you're listing your home because you just got your dream job across the state or country (or world). First, let me offer my congratulations! Now let's get down to the dirty business of relocation.

Staging and selling your home and the many memories it holds for you and your loved ones is tough. Let's face it, moving is a pain in the neck. I've done it enough times to know! Keeping unnecessary complications out of the picture is highly desirable. There are always surprises that will ambush you as you work your way through a real estate transaction, so why open yourself up more?

For those who buy their solar (with either cash or traditional financing), selling their home is straightforward, solar is just another home improvement that has value. If there is a loan balance outstanding, it is paid off in escrow.

The University of California, Berkeley did a study that looked at 70,000 home transactions to see whether solar panels had an impact on home value. They found that 'owned' solar added value to the home often in excess of the amount paid for the system. Imagine a home improvement that earns its keep as it goes being worth *more* when you sell your home – pretty sweet deal.

To the contrary, leased solar is not given the same consideration. You've already read what Fannie Mae and the FHA have to say about solar valuations (no value if leased), but what are the other risks associated with selling your home with leased solar panels on it?

Some real world examples are the best way I can think of to impart the very real downstream risks associated with leased solar panels if you ever choose to sell your home.

Risk #1: Your buyer doesn't qualify for the solar lease. You might be thinking to yourself, the buyer qualifies for a bank loan, why wouldn't they qualify to assume my lease payments?

Real world example 1:

A few years back, I was approached by a good friend who wanted to install solar panels on her house. She was having difficulty deciding between leasing and owning. At that time, I was unsure of the downstream implications of the solar leasing and didn't feel comfortable leasing her a system. Instead I presented her with a purchase option for a net cost (after incentives) of $16,000.

She eventually decided that she didn't want to come out of pocket any money and leased her system from a competitor. As a dyed in the wool salesman, losing any deal hurts, but losing one that close to home really stung. However, beyond my own pride, I worried about my friend and her husband. They were constantly talking about moving, and I knew that the lease could complicate their plans should they decide to get out of Dodge.

Sure enough, a year later, my friend's husband got his dream job and they had to relocate. They listed their home and got a great offer shortly thereafter, but their home nearly fell out of escrow on closing day because of a title issue. There was a lien on the property (UCC-1) against the solar equipment filed by the leasing company. Once alerted, the leasing company agreed to remove the lien, but because the buyer's fico score was below the 700 threshold they required, they were not approved to take over the lease, and the whole deal fell into question. These savvy buyers took advantage of this situation and reduced their offer by $16,000 (coincidence?), which my friends felt compelled to accept, and they got an even better deal on the house after their initial offer was accepted!

My friends' faced some terrible choices – buy out the solar lease for $48,000 (three times my original sale price!) or make the remainder of the $150/month lease payments for the next 19 years! Brutal!

Risk #2: The buyer isn't a lessee. By this I mean he/she doesn't lease stuff – cars, homes, anything.

As a group, they typically pay cash for everything. If this is your buyer, they've likely made a sweet cash offer on your home. You're stoked, because this means no banks, no appraisals, and a quick closing. All systems go! Except...

You have that leased solar system sitting up on your roof. "No problem," you think to yourself, "I remember the solar salesman explaining to me how everyone loves solar and how easy my lease would be to transfer to the next owner of my home."

Not so fast. Remember, this buyer doesn't lease anything. He's going to assume that the solar panels 'come with' the house, and when he finds out they don't, all bets are off. He'll demand you pay off the lease before he buys your home. Forget about countering, you'll have little luck raising the price now. You're stuck. My prediction, the deal falls out of escrow and the buyer walks. You suddenly find yourself in the unenviable position of selling your solar lease to the next sucker.

Real world example 2:

A good friend of mine in the solar industry just sold her home complete with a beautiful SunPower solar system on it. At appraisal time, because she owned the solar system, she received extra value ($25,000) for the solar and sold her home quickly without a hitch.

She and her husband immediately went shopping for a new home. Soon they found a one that they really liked and it even had a nice solar system on the roof to boot. As someone 'in the know' she inquired as to whether the system was leased or owned before she made an offer. At first, the seller's agent couldn't answer the question, but upon further investigation he disclosed that the solar panels were in fact leased. My colleague politely declined to make an offer and later found and bought an equivalent home without solar installed. They are in the process of installing an 'owned' system on their new home as I write this.

The lesson here is that when people 'in the biz' are passing on homes with leased solar panels on them, how long do you think it will be before everyone else follows suit?

Risk #3: The 'no fico score' buyer. This buyer is likely a foreign national who won't qualify to assume the lease because they literally don't have a fico score. They may or may not be opposed to leasing things, but it really doesn't matter because in the eyes of the leasing company, they are not qualified – period. No fico score = not qualified.

Your choices are: buy out the lease, keep making the payments for the remainder of the term, or walk away from the deal.

Risk #4: Real estate agents won't accept your listing. Sadly, this is happening more and more as additional paperwork and solar lien removals needlessly complicate their jobs. Many a real estate professional has been burned by tough to deal with solar leasing companies and simply won't take listings that include them anymore. Here's another example of you selling the lease only this time it's to the listing agent who would normally be beating down your door for your business. Where's that solar salesman when you need him?

He never told you you'd be doing his job if you ever tried to sell your home. Maybe it's time for you to go door to door...

Real world example 3:

I was recently speaking to a group of real estate agents about solar, specifically about how to market a home with solar panels installed on it. During the Q&A session, I received a slew of tough questions regarding solar leases and got the sense that these folks weren't fans. After my talk one agent, who had asked some particularly thorny questions, approached me and said, "You know, Scott, I just won't take them anymore."
"Take what?" I asked.
"I won't take listings with solar leases. They're just too much work. Buyers are getting wise to them and don't like them. They complicate the heck out of every sale and cause a lot of deals to fall apart. Why do people sign them in the first place?"
"To save money," I replied.
"Well, whatever they're saving ain't enough," he retorted.

Risk #5: The skinny buyer. I don't mean skinny in the physical sense. I mean skinny in the electron sense. This buyer uses way less electricity than you do, for illustrative purposes we'll say she uses half as much. This buyer is accustomed to paying low electric bills and isn't thinking much about them when she makes an offer on your house. The solar panels are attractive because she assumes she'll have no electric bill. Then you hit her with a $300/month solar lease payment that she has to take over if she wants the house. Houston, we have a problem, and it's this deal. Unless you can sell the lease, your home is back on the market.

Risk #6: The Repo. Believe it or not, today solar panels are being repossessed by leasing companies. Most often this occurs in a real estate transaction when the buyer doesn't want the panels or doesn't qualify to take over the lease and the seller defaults. To a lesser extent panels are repossessed when a home owner stops making payments. The repossession itself is expensive and ultimately the seller has to cough up cash or wind up in collections with a trashed FICO score.

Risk #7: The Move. Yup, you guessed it. You're taking the panels with you! The adoption fell through and you're stuck with the orphans.

Real world example 4:

We had a customer who leased a solar system and a couple years later sold his house to move into a larger one a couple miles away. The buyer qualified for the lease (good news), but refused to assume it (bad news). Since he had to buy it anyway, the seller decided to take the solar with him. The 4 kilowatt system ($15,000 after incentives if he bought it) ended up costing him $36,000 to buy out and another $7,000 to take off his roof, pack into a truck, and reinstall on his new house. In the end, he paid for that system just shy of three times.

Risk #8: Bad real estate market. There's really not much anyone can do if the market crashes. Whether you own the system or lease it, a down market is going to have a negative impact. The upside is that as long as you own the system, it's paying for room and board the entire time it lives on your roof, so if you sell in a down market, you'll at least recoup some of your investment. The longer you stay, the more you'll recoup. It's hard to know how leased solar will fare in a down market, but we can reasonably assume it won't do as well as its 'owned' counterpart since the buyer is holding all of the cards and doesn't have to do anything.

Real world example 5:

I bought my solar system in 2006. I paid off the loan I used to buy it by 2012 and have had several years of additional savings since. If I sell my house in a down market, I might not get much additional value, if any, for my solar panels, but I don't really need to since they've already paid for themselves plus another $8,000 in free electricity. I'm currently racking up free electricity to the tune of $3,000 a year. I've made my money back and then some. Any additional value is gravy.

If I had instead chosen to lease my system and the real estate market later tanked, I have to wonder who has the leverage in the sales transaction. Since a down market is usually defined as a buyers' market, by definition the seller is at a distinct disadvantage.

In a buyers' market, the seller generally has to make concessions in order to sell his home as motivated sellers outnumber picky buyers and the latter has her pick of the litter. The buyer has no motivation whatsoever to assume your solar lease, but you have every motivation to sell your house. What do you do? At this point, you're probably wishing you never answered the phone that fateful night the telemarketer convinced you to 'switch to solar and save'.

Some things to consider before you enter into a 20 year Marriage with a solar leasing company:

1. Will you be in your home for 20+ years? (This is a very long time to agree to anything!)
2. Will you sell in an up or down market? (really no way to know)
3. Will your buyer assume your lease payments? (not guaranteed)
4. What will you do if they don't? (buy it out, take it with you, default, or keep

making payments on a solar system installed on a house you no longer own)

PART 10:
PRENUPTIAL AGREEMENTS

When you take on project financing of any kind or don't disconnect from the electric grid entirely, you still have obligations you're responsible for. Since these are often contractual, you might think of them as prenuptial agreements.

A 'pre-nup', as it is commonly known, is a contractual arrangement that determines certain aspects of the marriage (financial and otherwise), but is generally most concerned with what happens when it ends. In the previous section we examined the risks related to how a solar leasing marriage might end if you decide to sell your home, but what if you stay in the house for the entire 20 year term?

With a loan, it's simple. At the end of the marriage, you own the solar system free and clear. After all, that's your arrangement with the bank, no? You pay them back all of their money (the principal) plus some interest and fees, and the solar system is yours, no questions asked. But what happens with leases and ppa's is quite different.

While the specifics can differ from lease to lease, generally, they all offer some version of the following options at the end of the term:

1. Purchase the system (that's right you don't own it even though you've paid for it for 20 years!). What you will pay for the solar panels after 20 years of making lease payments is pretty fuzzy, but it's often written in the contract as 'third party appraised value'. What does this mean exactly? Even we in the industry don't really know, but we generally agree that it won't be the scrap value or what you can sell the equipment for on EBay. The consensus opinion seems to be that the appraised value will be some multiple of the value of the electricity this 20 year old system is still producing. If the system was well built, it should still be producing 80% or more of what it did the day you turned it on. Let's say that 80% is 10,000 kilowatt hours per year and that a kilowatt hour is worth $0.75 (it is 20 years from now, so this is probably a

pretty conservative estimate). Using this formula, at a minimum, your system will be appraised for $7,500. However, since it theoretically has five more years of useful life left (due to the 25 year warranty), the appraiser may decide the system is worth a lot more than $7,500. Maybe even five times more! We won't know for sure until we get there, and in my opinion, that's quite a leap of faith for anyone to make.

2. Renew the lease/ppa for a period of time. Commonly you'll be allowed to do this for up to two more consecutive 'five year' terms and for a yet to be determined kilowatt hour rate. Do you really want to lease this thing for another ten years not knowing what the monthly payment will be?

3. Continue on a month to month basis at their discretion.

4. Remove the solar system. Some leases will remove the system and dispose of it at no cost to you, others will charge you some amount of money to be determined 20 years from now for the privilege, and still others may elect to abandon the system on your roof (in which case you'll be responsible for paying any taxes due when they 'transfer' the system to you). If you're considering a lease, read this part of the contract carefully so you will know what to expect when that day finally arrives.

5. If you elect to remove the solar system, some leases promise to return your roof to a pre-solar watertight condition while others expressly state they are not responsible for doing this. If you lease, you obviously want to go with the company that is contractually obligated to respect your roof.

6. Balloon payment. In addition to a third party appraised value, you may be responsible for a balloon payment at the end of the lease. This is often referred to as the system's 'residual value'. Tread cautiously here. This a way for the solar salesman to jack up the price of your solar panels while keeping your monthly payments attractively low. The language in the contract usually states that the buyout price of the system in year 20 is the higher of the 'residual value' *or* the third party appraised value. For the leasing company, the residual value locks a guaranteed minimum buyout price. Check your payment schedule carefully to avoid this cleverly disguised time bomb.

Familiarizing yourself with your end of lease options is critical to avoiding unpleasant surprises later. It's time well spent and can save you tens of thousands of dollars and a priceless amount of hassle!

The other part of your prenuptial obligation is with The Electric Company (unless you're entirely off-grid). The contract that governs your responsibilities here is call a Net Metering Agreement. This document lays out everything you must do to interconnect your solar panels with The Electric Company's grid including carrying homeowner's insurance, installing an inverter that is grid compliant, allowing access to your solar system to shut it down (for maintenance), etc.

This is a non-negotiable contract. If you don't sign it, you can't connect your solar system to the grid. If you don't abide by it, The Electric Company can shut your system off.

The good news is that net metering agreements are focused on safety and interoperability standards. There's very little chance you'll ever find yourself on the wrong side of one unless you do something really, really dumb, and then you'll probably be a candidate for a Darwin Award.

PART 11:

REMARRYING VS. DATING

With your divorce from The Electric Company now behind you, should you rush out and get remarried or do some casual dating? For most of us, the answer would most definitely be the latter, though there's no telling with some people.

I define remarrying, for the purposes of this book, as the act of entering into some long term energy contract with penalties due if and when you choose to end it. While your divorce from The Electric Company was relatively painless (unless you selected a bad contractor), your divorce from a solar leasing company could be very expensive or not depending upon your timing and your luck.

I've covered the in's and out's, pitfalls, and traps of leases in a fair amount of detail in this book, but it's worth noting that entering into a 20 year commitment with a financing company is a lot like getting remarried.

My advice to you is to tread carefully and read the contracts thoroughly before you put pen to paper. Know the terms of their prenuptial agreement, how much it might cost you to exit, and what your options are should your new spouse not want to remarry your home's new buyer (or vice-a-versa).

In my opinion, signing a solar lease (especially if you agree to a 'tier shaver' – an arrangement where you still end up paying a portion of your traditional electric bill plus the lease payment) is like getting remarried, but letting your ex stay in the spare bedroom.

I'm sure that the lead generator at Big Box Hardware didn't explain it to you in quite this fashion, but you can't really blame him, he's probably inexperienced and has received very little training.

What if, God forbid, you actually get divorced from your actual human spouse with a solar lease attached to your home? Which one of you signed it? That person is ultimately the one who is responsible for dealing with it. If you choose to lease, make sure all parties sign the contract, so should you decide to split up, you'll still be dealing with this together.

Getting a home improvement loan or traditional financing, on the other hand, is more like going steady than getting married. Sure, there's a contract, and you're on the hook for paying the money back, but if you borrow right, your loan will be free of prepayment penalties and other booby traps. It will provide you with positive cash flow from day one, and when you sell your home, the loan will be paid off in escrow. If you pay it off early, you own the solar system free and clear and everyone goes on with their lives, no harm, no foul.

PART 12:
SOLAR AND YOUR FUTURE

Congratulations! You've made it to the end of the main section of this book. You now know more than 99% of the solar salespeople you'll encounter on your quest to divorce The Electric Company. Leveraging the techniques I've revealed here can save you thousands and possibly tens of thousands of dollars on equipment, fees, financing, and penalties, as well as, help you to avoid second rate gear, shady contractors, and financing headaches.

I hope that my warnings and cautionary tales didn't spook you so much that you no longer want to go solar. That was not my intention. I simply wish to convey how a simple home improvement has been needlessly overcomplicated by an industry still searching to find itself.

I experience immense joy every time I see a new, well installed solar system find a good home. I am inspired by all of you who share my passion for a greener, cleaner planet. Solar energy is fast becoming cheap and ubiquitous, and not a moment too soon.

Thomas Edison once said, "We are like tenant farmers chopping down the fence around our house for fuel when we should be using Nature's inexhaustible sources of energy — sun, wind and tide. ... I'd put my money on the sun and solar energy. What a source of power! I hope we don't have to wait until oil and coal run out before we tackle that."

Well, you don't have to wait any longer, solar is here, and in a big way. You'll save money – lots of it over your solar panels' useful life – and reduce your footprint on our planet in the process. Your savings are tax free (no one can tax the sun or savings) and will increase year after year as the cost of electricity continues to rise and the number of addictive electronic devices in our lives continue to multiply.

If you haven't done so already, someday you'll acquire an electric vehicle and kiss your gasoline bills goodbye, too, or take your excess solar electricity, direct it into a hydrolyzer and make your own hydrogen fuel from tap water.

Where you go from here, is up to you, but at least you've acquired the knowledge you need to do it right, do it well, and save a ton of money! I hope you take what you've learned from this book and share it with others. My goal in writing it was to help folks like you avoid the snake oil salesman and shady financing products that have become so pervasive in the solar industry today. Please do your part and help others to go solar the right way! Share this book with them!

I wish you the best of luck on your journey. May the rest of your days be forever sunny.

GLOSSARY OF SOLAR TERMS

While I've introduced a lot of industry specific terms throughout this book, there are many I didn't have time to cover. I've included those here along with many you have already read about. Consider this section a quick reference guide in the event that your solar salesman hits you with solar vocabulary you may not be familiar with.

Alternating Current – More commonly known as AC. This is the type of electricity that powers the grid and your home.

Array – A grouping of solar panels. Panels spread across three roofs would commonly be described as three arrays while a solar system on a single roof would be described a single array.

Azimuth – Direction, as in north, south, east, west or some variant thereof.

Balance of System – Or B.O.S., is all of the wire, conduit, electrical breakers, nuts, bolts, roof sealant, flashings, etc. required to put a solar array together and interconnect it with the grid.

Battery – A chemical device used to store electricity.

Charge Controller – A piece of power electronics that controls the rate at which batteries charge.

Critical Loads Panel – This is a subpanel that contains all of your home's critical power needs as defined by you. Generally installed in conjunction with a battery backup system or generator.

Day Laborers – Often Illegal and uninsured workers used by shady contractors to cut corners.

Delivery Charges – The cost of delivering electricity to your home over the transmission lines.

Demand Charge – A fee determined by the amount of electricity (kilowatts) used during any fifteen minute period of time in a single billing cycle.

Direct Current – Commonly called DC, is the type of electricity created by solar panels and stored in batteries.

Do Not Call Registry – A national registry of people who have elected to opt out of receiving annoying telemarketing calls.

Energy Audit – Something every savvy solar customer does before he begins shopping for solar panels.

Energy Efficient – A state of mind. The more energy efficient you are the less money you spend on solar panels.

Escalator – The amount your lease, ppa, or solar loan payment is scheduled to increase annually.

Feed-in-Tariff – A predetermined sum paid for the electricity generated from a renewable energy system. Also called FITs, they are a type of incentive for installing solar panels in some states.

Generation Charges – The cost of creating electricity at the power plant.

Grid – The electrical infrastructure the delivers power to end users.

Incentives – Local, state, and federal rebates, credits, Feed-in-Tariffs, and RECs that discount the cost of solar energy.

Inverter – The device the takes the energy from a solar panel and converts it to grid compliant AC.

Islanding – A state where your home's solar energy system operates independently from the grid. Grid compliant inverters have an anti-islanding feature (meaning they shut off when the electric grid goes down) to protect linemen and other workers. True islanding requires a battery bank and an islanding inverter.

Kilowatt hour – one thousand watts used over the course of a single hour. For example, a 100 watt lightbulb running for 10 hours consumes one kilowatt hour or one kWh.

Lease – A way to rent your solar panels. Terms vary from ten to twenty-five years.

LEDs – light emitting diodes, aka super energy efficient lightbulbs.

License – Something every contractor you hire has to have legally to perform work on your property.

Lien – A legal filing on your property's title that secures a financier's interest in their solar asset.

Megawatt – One thousand kilowatts

Megawatt hour – One thousand kilowatt hours

Micro Inverter – A type of inverter that attaches directly to a solar panel in a one-to-one relationship.

Module – Industry jargon for solar panel

Monitoring – The act of recording and measuring solar energy output and system health over time by way of a data collection device and web portal.

Net metering – The state of connecting to the grid and 'spinning your meter backwards' for credits.

Notice to Proceed – Or NTP, is permission granted by the financing company to the contractor to begin building the solar project.

O&M – Operations and Maintenance. This is the ongoing care and feeding of a solar energy system over time.

Optimizer – Similar to a micro inverter except the DC to AC conversion occurs in a centralized inverter instead of at the panel level.

P.A.C.E. – Property Assessed Clean Energy. A method of financing energy efficiency improvements through your property taxes.

Permission to Operate – Also called PTO is permission granted by The Electric Company to activate your solar energy system and connect it to the grid.

Pooky – Industry slang for roof sealant.

Power Purchase Agreement – Or PPA is an arrangement where you agree to buy the electricity a solar system creates at a prearranged price per kilowatt hour. Terms typically run 20 years and generally contain payment escalators.

Production Guarantee – A guaranteed refund for every kilowatt below the solar system's annual production estimate.

REC – Renewable Energy Credit is a type of financial incentive that typically represents payment for one megawatt hour of energy production from a renewable energy system.

Robo Dialer – The computer that keeps calling your house over and over again until you answer. See Do not Call Registry.

Service Entrance – Your main electrical panel generally located next to the utility meter.

Shading – The number one way to reduce your solar system's output.

Slope – The tilt or angle of the solar panels relative to the sun.

Smart Grid – A bidirectional grid that intelligently delivers electricity from node of generation to nodes of demand.

Smart Meter – The Electric Company's digital meter that records your electricity consumption in 15 minute usage intervals. They allow for remote billing, service activation/deactivation, monitoring, and new utility billing structures.

Soiling – The dirt and debris that collects on solar modules over time.

Strip and Comp – A construction practice of removing brittle roofing material (clay tile, lightweight concrete, slate, wood shake, etc), installing asphalt shingles, installing the panels on the shingles, and 'framing up' the installation with the original roofing materials. Considered an industry best practice for brittle/fragile roofs.

Transfer – The act of transitioning your lease or ppa obligations to another party.

Third Party Appraised Value – The manner in which the buyout of a solar lease or ppa is determined.

Tiered Rates – A tariff structure designed to charge ever increasing rates for electricity in a stair step fashion. The more electricity you use, the more you pay for each unit. So much for buying in bulk!

Tier Shaver – A solar system that only addresses only the upper most expensive utility rate tiers.

Time of Use – Or TOU is a billing structure that charges different rates based on time of day and time of year.

True-up – The annual bill from The Electric Company based on the amount of energy you used subtracted from the amount of energy you generated or vise-a-versa depending on individual consumption habits. Produce more than you consume and you get a credit. Do the opposite and you get a bill.

ADDITIONAL RESOURCES

This section provides additional independent resources that will help you dig deeper into various topics related to energy efficiency, rebates, contractor selection, and solar financing.

Energy Efficiency Resources:

http://energy.gov/energysaver/energy-saver

http://www.ase.org/resources/top-10-home-energy-efficiency-tips

http://www.goodhousekeeping.com/home/g2359/energy-saving-tips/

http://www.energystar.gov/index.cfm?c=products.pr_save_energy_at_home

Solar Incentives and Rebate Programs:

http://www.dsireusa.org/

http://energy.gov/savings

http://www.irs.gov/pub/irs-pdf/f5695.pdf

Contractor Selection:

http://www.consumerreports.org/cro/home-garden/resource-center/choosing-a-contractor/overview/index.htm

https://www.sba.gov/content/choosing-contractor

http://www.consumer.ftc.gov/articles/0242-hiring-contractor

Solar Financing:

http://www.consumer.ftc.gov/articles/0532-solar-power-your-home#Leases

http://www.ksl.com/?sid=35139419&nid=1268&scid=rss-extlink

http://www.solarfeeds.com/buying-vs-leasing-solar/

Comprehensive Guide to Financing Solar by the National Renewable Energy Laboratory (NREL):

http://www.nrel.gov/docs/fy99osti/26242.pdf

ABOUT THE AUTHOR

Scott Gordon is President of HelioPower, an integrated energy services company based in California. Scott began shopping for solar for his own home in 2006 before becoming one of the first consumers to participate in the California Solar Initiative. He later went on to sell residential and commercial solar energy, battery storage, and predictive analytics to clients in the Southwestern United States as he ascended the corporate ladder. With over 5,000 solar energy installations under his belt, Scott has been invited to speak on a variety of renewable energy related topics including: Energy Efficiency for Homeowners, The Ugly Side of Solar, Grid 3.0 – The Future of Energy, Solar Energy Finance for Beginners, Residential Solar Sales for Newbies, and Intro to Solar Energy Concepts. He is also co-author of *The Tinker and The Fold,* a Sci-fi novel he co-wrote with his son Evan to explore moral and ethical issues related to the way humans treat the planet and each other. He lives with his wife and three children in Orange County, CA.